Rookie
Read-About Science®

Knowing about Noses

WITHDRAWN

By Allan Fowler

Consultants
Linda Cornwell, Learning Resource Consultant,
Indiana Department of Education

Sharyn Fenwick, Elementary Science/Math Specialist
Gustavus Adolphus College, St. Peter, Minnesota

Janann V. Jenner, Ph.D.

CP Children's Press®
A Division of Grolier Publishing
New York   London   Hong Kong   Sydney
Danbury, Connecticut

Visit Children's Press® on the Internet at:
http://publishing.grolier.com

Designer: Herman Adler Design Group

Library of Congress Cataloging-in-Publication Data

Fowler, Allan.
　　Knowing about noses / by Allan Fowler.
　　　　p. cm. – (Rookie read-about science)
　　Includes index.
　　Summary: Describes the noses of different animals and how they are used.
　　ISBN 0-516-20810-1 (lib. bdg.)　　　0-516-26480-X (pbk.)
　　1. Nose—Juvenile literature. [1. Nose. 2. Animals—Physiology.]
　　I. Title. II. Series.
　　QM505.F68　　1999　　　　　　　　　　　　　　97-31279
　　573.8'77—dc21　　　　　　　　　　　　　　　　　CIP
　　　　　　　　　　　　　　　　　　　　　　　　　　AC

Wow! What a nose this proboscis (pra-BOS-kes) monkey has! "Proboscis" is a fancy word for nose. It's easy to see how the monkey got its name!

Most monkeys and apes, such as gorillas, have flat noses.

A baboon's nose is at the end of a long snout, like a dog's nose.

Look at the nose of a wild boar. You can tell it belongs to the pig family.

A pig's snout ends
in a flat nose.

Humans use their noses for smelling and breathing.

Dog noses sense smells
that human noses can't.
A beagle can follow the trail
of a person just by smell.

To a dog, no two
people smell alike.

Do you have a dog? If you do, your dog may bark and run toward the door to greet you even before you enter the house.

That is because your dog knows your smell. Dogs can also smell things from far away.

You might not think fish
can smell things underwater,
but many of them can.

Sharks often find
their prey by smell.

Fish don't breathe through noses like most land animals do.

They breathe through gills on the sides of their bodies.

Noses are sometimes noisy. Horses snort through their noses.

Elephants trumpet
through their trunks.

A trunk is a long nose
that hangs down.

Tapirs (TAY-pirs) have trunks.

So do elephant seals.
They are called elephant
seals because they have
trunks like elephants.

Of course their trunks are much shorter than those of elephants. An elephant's trunk is the longest nose on any animal.

An elephant sucks up
water with its trunk. Then
it squirts the water into its
mouth to drink or onto its
back to shoo away flies.

An elephant uses its trunk
to pick up food to eat.

An elephant can even
do a hard day's work
with its nose.

It can pick up logs
or other heavy objects.

Aren't you lucky that
you have hands to do
those things?

It leaves your nose
free for breathing, for
smelling, and sometimes
for sneezing!

Words You Know

snout

trunk

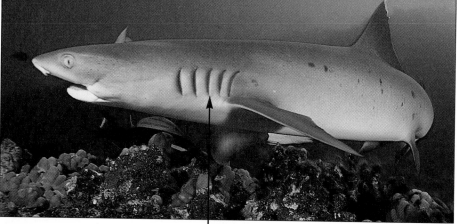

gills

beagle

gorilla

proboscis monkey

tapir

Index

About the Author

Allan Fowler is a freelance writer with a background in advertising.
Born in New York, he now lives in Chicago and enjoys traveling.

Photo Credits

©: Photo Researchers: 12 (Art Attack), cover (Holt Studios International
Andrew Morant), 5 (Tim Davis), 26 (Sven O. Lindblad), 22 (C.K. Lorenz),
10, 31 top left (Renee Lynn), 3, 31 bottom left (S.R. Maglione), 15 (Frederick
R. McConnaughey), 9 (Joseph Nettis), 19 (Chobe N. Park), 6, 7, 30 top left
(Hans Reinhard); Visuals Unlimited: 24 (Don W. Fawcett), 17, 30 bottom
(David B. Fleetham), 25 (John Gerlach), 11 (Arthur R. Hill), 18 (Corinne
Humphrey), 20, 31 bottom right (Mike Long), 4, 14, 31 top right (Ken Lucas),
21 (Erwin C. Bud Nielson/Images International), 23, 30 top right (Kjell B.
Sandved), 29 (William J. Weber).